HEARING VOICES

To Mike
Best Wishes for

ALSO BY CLARE SUMMERSKILL

Books
We're the Girls (Diana Publishing, 2008)

Short Stories
"Single Again", *Diva Book of Short Stories*,
ed. Helen Sandler (Diva, 2000)
"Maggie Maybe", *Groundswell*, ed. Helen Sandler (Diva, 2002)

Plays
Gateway to Heaven (2006)
Once Upon a Lifetime (2002)
An Evening with Katie's Gang (2000)

Filmscripts
Gateway to Heaven (2007)
Queens' Evidence (2009)

CDs
Make It Sound Easy
Feels Like Coming Home
Still Let Me Fly

Orders and other inquiries to: admin@claresummerskill.co.uk
Websites: www.claresummerskill.co.uk
www.hearingvoicesplay.co.uk

HEARING VOICES

A PLAY BY

Clare Summerskill

First published by Tollington Press, London, 2010
www.tollingtonpress.co.uk

Copyright © Clare Summerskill 2010

Clare Summerskill has asserted her rights under the
Copyright, Design & Patents Act 1988 to be identified as
the author of this work.

A catalogue record for this book is available from
the British Library.

ISBN 978-0-9560173-3-8

Cover design by Natasha Coverdale
Typeset by Helen Sandler

Printed in Great Britain by the MPG Books Group,
Bodmin and King's Lynn

Mixed Sources
Product group from well-managed
forests and other controlled sources
www.fsc.org Cert no. TT-COC-002303
© 1996 Forest Stewardship Council
FSC

AUTHOR'S NOTE

This play has been written entirely from interviews with people with whom I was in hospital as well as certain professionals who offer alternative ideas on how people in mental distress can be cared for and insights into why staff in the current NHS psychiatric system treat patients the way they do. These interviews have been woven around my own account of my stay in hospital. Aside from my story, everything else that is said in the play has been said, word for word, by one of the interviewees. Names of hospitals, wards and some individuals have been changed or omitted in this publication.

Clare Summerskill

CONTRIBUTORS

PAM BLACKWOOD was head of operations with Samaritans between 2003 and 2009 and was also a member of the Guideline Development Group for the 2005 NICE Report on Self-Harm.

DR RUFUS MAY works as a clinical psychologist in Bradford. He was once diagnosed as a "paranoid schizophrenic" but hasn't taken any medication in twenty-two years.

DR RACHEL PERKINS is a clinical psychologist and director of quality assurance and user experience in South West London and St George's Mental Health NHS Trust. She is a member of the Disability Rights Commission's Mental Health Advisory Group and a trustee of Rethink. She is a user of mental health services as she has bipolar disorder.

PADDY BAZELEY was one of the founding directors of Maytree, a sanctuary for the suicidal in London where people can stay up to four nights at no cost. Maytree is run by a few full-time people and over sixty volunteers.

DEB ELTHALION is a singer and musician and mother of five who has bipolar disorder.

EILEEN, ALISON, MARY and TONY have all given their permission for their testimonies to be used in this play.

CLARE SUMMERSKILL is a stand-up, a singer/songwriter and a playwright. www.claresummerskill.co.uk

CAST

Actress 1: CLARE

Actor 1: Dr RUFUS MAY, TONY, CONSULTANT, EXERCISE MAN, KEVIN

Actress 2: EILEEN, ALISON, SUSAN, SARAH, DR RACHEL PERKINS, PAM BLACKWOOD

Actress 3: MARY, DEBBIE, PADDY BAZELEY, MATILDA, CLAUDIA, GLADYS, ANGELA, YVONNE

Other parts (NURSE, PATIENT, etc) are played by Actor 1, Actress 2 and Actress 3.

HEARING VOICES

ACT ONE

Scene One

CLARE: For two years I had been feeling suicidal and I was
exhausted. I had been living in a world with no joy, no
hope and my only thoughts were about how to stop all
this pain and end my life.

I went to Paris on my own for a holiday, hoping that
the beauty of that city and the contents of its galleries
and museums might somehow calm my troubled
mind. But you know that Van Gogh painting? The
one of his room with a bed and a wicker chair and the
perspective's at a slant? That one? Well there I was,
looking at it in the Musée d'Orsay, and the objects in
the picture started sort of coming out at me, like it was
3D. And at that moment I understood that the painter
had clearly been mad and I could now see that madness
in his work and amongst the bright and vivid colours
I could also see his pain. And then I looked at some of
the other Van Goghs and they all seemed to be coming
away from the wall, calling for my attention and I
began to freak, because it was like hallucinating and it
was at that moment that I knew what this all meant…
that I was maybe going where he had been.

Over the next few weeks things went from bad to worse
until one morning I made an appointment with my

GP and asked for some sleeping pills. Then I went back home and I took the whole packet. I remember running out of water, there were so many pills to swallow, and having to fill the glass up again, and then I sat down on my bed, thinking, "I've finally had the courage to do it. Peace at long last!"

That done, I laid me down to die and I remember that bit being wonderful... I was so tired, so low, so empty of any kind of hope that things could ever improve and it was such a relief to stop struggling and to finally give up the fight.

I could feel myself slipping into a seductive state of unconsciousness when, completely on the spur of the moment, I decided to call my therapist. I didn't think of it as a cry for help, I thought it was too late for that, I just wanted to explain to her what I had done and why and to say sorry that I didn't have the strength to keep battling on.

THERAPIST: Hi. I can't take your call at the moment but leave a message and I'll get back to you just as soon as I can.

CLARE: It's me. I just wanted to say "goodbye" and thank you for all your support. I'm so sorry, I'm really sorry.

But the reason I'm still here to tell my tale is because she phoned me back a few hours later, got no reply because I was unconscious and she then called the police who sent the fire brigade round to my flat to break in and rescue me.

But I knew nothing about all that. A day and a half later I vaguely remember being at a general hospital and I was then transferred to a secure psychiatric wing at another hospital in central London.

You know what has always moved me? The kindness of strangers.

ACTOR: The kindness of strangers, part one.

CLARE: When I arrived there one of the ambulance men
helped me out of the van because I was so weak and as
we walked towards the ward I sort of squeezed his hand.
He held it tightly and then squeezed it back supportively.
I think he was trying to give me a little encouragement
for the journey which he knew lay ahead.

After a five-minute medical examination I was shown
to a room and left there on one of the beds. I found out
that the woman I was sharing with was called Alison
and we have stayed in touch ever since.

ALISON: I've been on that ward several times before.
Once when I was a patient there I had leave to go out
for a walk and I tried to commit suicide by jumping
off Westminster Bridge into the River Thames. I heard
voices and the voices were saying:

VOICE: *(From man walking behind Alison)* You're going to be
butchered in bed if you don't jump into the Thames.

ALISON: I was very, very, very depressed at the time and I
didn't mind the thought of dying so I jumped into the
river but it's not very deep so I didn't drown. The police
picked me up and put silver paper round me to keep me
warm and then they took me back to the ward.

CLARE: And is that why you were in hospital when I was
there?

ALISON: No, after that first time I tried to commit suicide
again 'cos I was still very depressed. I tried to jump

under a train. I just wanted to end it all. It was at King's
Cross. It wasn't very busy. There weren't many people
on the platform so I went to the end, right down to the
end of the platform. I fell under the railway lines so
they stopped the train and turned all the power off.

They crawled underneath the train. It was quite some
feat and I crawled out between the carriages and a
paramedic came through with a member of staff to
see if I'd broken anything. They put me on a stretcher
and carried me up the escalator and they took me to
hospital. They cut all my clothes off and tested me to
see if I'd done anything to my back, which I hadn't. I
was all intact but I had a bruise on my leg. Then I was
taken over to the ward.

CLARE: So when you jumped on the track, was that
    because you heard voices?

ALISON: No, it wasn't voices. It was me that time.

CLARE: What was different from the time you jumped off
    the bridge?

ALISON: I thought it would work. I was convinced it would
    work. I would just be mown down and that would be
    the end of me, but it wasn't. I fell in the gap.

CLARE: And why did you want it to end?

ALISON: 'Cos I was really depressed and I saw no hope for
    the future.

CLARE: So how do you feel about it being unsuccessful?

ALISON: I was disappointed at the time. But now I'm quite
    pleased. Quite pleased I survived.

Scene Two

CLARE: Just a week before the overdose I'd been acting in a national tour of a play that I'd written but now I was a bona fide loony on a secure psychiatric ward where I was kept for two months because they thought that I was still at risk from killing myself.

I look back on that time and I don't think that I was really mad. I was definitely ill, I don't doubt that, but was I mad? Can someone be mad and then later on be sane? I don't know... but let me tell you that it's really hard to admit that I was what some people might call "mad", even just for a while. It's actually a bit like coming out all over again... but even harder because your mother can't blame it all on your games teacher! But I'm OK now! I'm almost completely mended. Nearly back to normal. And I'm ready to tell you my story.

The first few days in hospital were all a bit of a blur, but I do remember begging the nurses to have a room of my own. It wasn't a "Virginia Woolf" thing; it was just that I felt this strong need to be somehow contained, by four solid walls, or by someone, but just to be contained.

Finally they gave me a single room but as I moved my stuff across the corridor I realised that I was missing Alison already. Maybe I shouldn't be alone. Maybe it was good to have someone else there.

As we entered the room I remember saying to a nurse:

What's that on the ceiling?

NURSE: What's what?

CLARE: Up there, on the ceiling. Is that blood?

NURSE: No.

CLARE: Why's there blood up there?

NURSE: Don't you be worrying about that.

CLARE: A leaflet was put down on my bedside table. I wasn't really up to reading any sort of literature at that point but I kept it and finally got around to looking at it a few months later. It said:

ACTOR: *(With leaflet)* Welcome to Elliott Tillery Ward!

CLARE: Oh, thank you. That's nice!

ACTOR: A leaflet provided for the patients by the staff!

CLARE: In general I think that most of the patients there, including myself, were pretty unaware of much that was going on around them in their first few days on the ward. But if we had been able to read the leaflet we would have seen that it said:

ACTOR: *(Very loud and cheery)* Welcome to Elliott Tillery Ward!

CLARE: Which made it sound like a bit like Butlins!

ACTOR: By now you should have been familiarised with the ward...

CLARE: I was certainly familiarised with the securely locked door at the end of the corridor and another locked door behind it and I knew that I was not allowed out through them but I had been told nothing about how anything worked on the ward or how long I might be there.

I remember that all I had to wear on the first night was a hospital regulation nightshirt; you know, the kind that doesn't do up at the back. I had a small bag with me but no extra clothes. Alison told me:

ALISON: Don't leave anything out, or even on your sink because people nick things.

CLARE: What kind of things?

ALISON: Toothpaste, soap, anything. When I leave my room I take all my important belongings.

CLARE: And she did! She took this bag with her every time she went to the loo or for a fag.

I was told by another patient that there was a ward safe where I could put any valuables should I want to. I had my driving licence in my wallet and I decided to ask the staff to look after that. I filled out a slip and then they took it off somewhere. A couple of weeks later there was a form that I needed to complete about a benefit claim and it asked if I had any proof of identity.

(To NURSE) Excuse me, could I please have my driving licence back?

NURSE: Where did you put it?

CLARE: I gave it to a nurse to put in the ward safe or wherever you keep valuables.

NURSE: We don't have a safe on the ward.

CLARE: But I've got a piece of paper here saying that you took it!

NURSE looks at form

NURSE: I've never seen a form like this...

CLARE: Well could you try and find out where my licence has gone please?

NURSE: I'm busy right now. I'll look into it later...

NURSE walks off

CLARE: But I kept asking for it and the next day another nurse appeared with my licence in a plastic bag. Hurrah!

NURSE: Now what do you need this for?

CLARE: I just need something to prove my identity. Thanks.

NURSE: I can't give you this.

CLARE: Why not?

NURSE: Because you're not allowed to drive while you're on a psychiatric ward.

CLARE: But I don't want to drive.

NURSE: So why do you want the licence?

CLARE: Because I've been filling out this form that says I need identification. I don't want to drive anywhere and even if I did, I wouldn't actually need that licence to do so, would I? I could just drive anyway.

NURSE: But you're not allowed to drive... not while you're on the ward.

CLARE: Listen to me carefully... I DON'T WANT TO DRIVE! I JUST WANT MY LICENCE BACK!

PAUSE

One of the places that the staff seldom entered was the smoking room. It was horrible there and when you entered, the smoke that filled it caught you like a pair of strong hands around your throat. There were a few metal chairs welded to the floor and a plant in the corner with three leaves on it. Like many of us, it was just about holding onto the struggle for life...

I didn't smoke myself but I was in there one day on my own just looking across the river at the Houses of Parliament. I come from a family of politicians who had spent their lives working in those very buildings, voting on national issues, making laws.

ACTOR: Order, order! This house must come to order!

CLARE: And I had even given an after-dinner speech myself at an event at the House of Lords about a year previously. But now here I was, on the other side of the river, on the other side of the fence... Behind reinforced windows that couldn't be opened more than an inch, looking across at those beautiful and historical buildings.

I thumped the glass in frustration and despair. Well, it wasn't really glass, it was a very strong plastic and I thumped it again until my hand started hurting. I was stuck in here and the rest of the world was going about its everyday business, working in the Commons and the Lords, driving buses across the bridge, strolling along the

Embankment and here I was, imprisoned on a psychiatric ward. How had this come about and how had I deserved it? I suddenly felt overtaken by a furious rage.

ACTOR: Dr Rachel Perkins is a clinical psychologist and director of quality assurance and user experience in South West London and St Georges Mental Health NHS Trust.

DR RACHEL: I'm a member of the Disability Rights Commission's Mental Health Advisory Group and a trustee of Rethink and I'm a user of mental health services because I have bipolar disorder... I just go mad every now and then and I go into hospital every couple of years!

In hospital people do become angry and aggressive. I think of mental health problems as a kind of bereavement because you lose the privileges of sanity, and anger – fury – is a normal response to bereavement.

CLARE: Thump, against the window. Thump against the injustice. Thump against all those who had no idea what I was going through in here. Thump against the person I might have been if I wasn't the person I now was... the person thumping windows until the side of her hand was bruised and aching with pain.

DR RACHEL: To be angry that the world's done this to you is a perfectly ordinary thing. It's not because you're ill that you're angry, it's because something devastating's happening to you. So you've lost the privileges of freedom but you've also lost the right to be believed.

CLARE: Since my admission a few days previously no-one had explained to me whether I had been sectioned or if I was a voluntary patient or who to ask what I was or what those terms even meant. If I had been at all able to read and digest…

ACTOR: The Elliott Tillery Ward leaflet…

CLARE: It might have made at least a few things slightly clearer:

ACTOR: (*Cheery*) We thought you would like to have some further information about life on the ward! Your consultant is the doctor responsible for your care and you will be able to discuss your medication and treatment, your leave time and your future discharge plans when you meet at the ward round.

CLARE: Everyone was constantly using this term "ward round" and I eventually found out that it meant when the patients get to see a psychiatrist. I arrived at the hospital on the Thursday but the next ward round wasn't till the following Monday, which meant that for four days I was there with no one to explain what the plan of my stay or my treatment was.

The consultant psychiatrists, as I found out, were the generals and the nurses were their trusty foot soldiers, supposedly carrying out their orders to the letter. Nothing could be done regarding your medication or your leave or when you were getting out until the consultant said so. When it came to seeing him (and it always was a "him"), I wasn't even told that was what was happening. A nurse came into my room and said:

NURSE: Come.

CLARE: Just like that! I didn't know where she wanted me to go so I waited for some explanation.

NURSE: *(More forcefully)* Come!

CLARE: Come where?

NURSE: *(Beckoning)* COME!

CLARE: I followed her down the corridor and through one of the locked doors and into a room where there were several people sitting round a table looking at me like I was some kind of biological specimen.

CONSULTANT: Hello... *(Looking at notes and reading)* erm... Clare, how are you?

CLARE: OK, thank you.

CONSULTANT: And what is your mood?

CLARE: I'm sorry?

CONSULTANT: Your mood, today. What is your mood?

CLARE: I don't really know what you mean by that?

CONSULTANT: Your mood. Is it high or low?

CLARE: Well, low I suppose.

CONSULTANT: We're going to put you on some anti-depressants and some diazepam three times a day and see how that works and some zopiclone for the night-time.

CLARE: I'd prefer not to have those ones 'cos they're what I overdosed on.

CONSULTANT: Oh, I see.

CLARE: I've actually been in therapy for a while and my therapist said that she would really like to talk to you if that would be possible?

CONSULTANT: We don't usually do that. Perhaps we could erm… take her number from you at some point and then if we have time to call her…

CLARE: *(To audience)* But they never did.

CONSULTANT: We'll see you again in a few days.

CLARE: A very long time ago in what seemed like another lifetime I had been commissioned to write a play for an NHS nurses' conference and from somewhere at the back of my mind I recalled that old joke:

"What's the difference between God and a consultant? God doesn't think that he's a consultant!"

NURSE: Come.

ACTOR: *(Cheery voice)* Your allocated nurse varies each shift and you can find out who he… stroke she… is from the whiteboard on the wall by the office.

CLARE: There was indeed a board by the office, and twice a day with great aplomb someone would come out and write the names of nurses next to the names of patients. One day I noticed that they'd spelt my name slightly wrong. They'd written "Claire" with an "i". Well I'm sorry but even through the haze of my mental illness I still felt that in terms of serious threats to our civilisation, after global warming and world poverty, incorrect spelling probably comes a close third. So I went over to the board and with one finger I simply removed the offending letter from my name.

A NURSE leaps on CLARE and forcibly pulls her away

NURSE: Don't touch that! Come away from there. Don't you ever touch that again.

CLARE: I later found out from other patients that the board was there to let the patients know who their so-called "named nurse" was that day. But during my stay on that ward no member of staff ever explained to me what a "named nurse" actually was or told me that they were one.

One evening, however, one of the nurses did come into my room to talk to me. She sat down on the chair opposite my bed and asked:

MATILDA: How are you doing?

CLARE: Well, no other nurse had inquired how I was since I'd been there so I thought that was quite nice of her.

MATILDA: You don't want to be harming yourself. Things are never that bad.

CLARE: What's your name?

MATILDA: Matilda.

CLARE: She seemed kind enough.

MATILDA: You know, the other night I went past my son's bedroom and I heard him crying so I went into his room.

CLARE: Oh, poor thing.

MATILDA: I took his hand in mine and we both knelt down on the floor and I prayed to God that he would take my son's pain away. That's what I do, when I'm down, I pray to the Lord and ask for his forgiveness and then I open the Bible at any page, and what I read there will show me the way through the problem and make me feel better... I think you should kneel down, Clare, and pray too.

CLARE: Thank you and I'm glad that it helps you but I'm not actually a Christian.

MATILDA: Just kneel down before the Lord and ask for his forgiveness.

CLARE: OK. Thanks. I'll bear that in mind.

MATILDA: And he will make you strong.

CLARE: Right... so your son, the other night...

MATILDA: Yes?

CLARE: Did you find out what was wrong, why he was crying in the first place?

MATILDA: No, but we prayed together before the Lord and read the Bible and I think that if you did that too it would make you feel better.

CLARE: Oh. OK.

MATILDA: Good night then.

CLARE: Good night Matilda.

MATILDA EXITS

I did not believe this to be an example of the kindness of strangers...

Scene Three

CLARE: Before I took the overdose I had never had any sort of
mental illness but the break-up of a long-term relationship
had sent me off the rails and into what my therapist had
explained was some very old trauma from my childhood
which had resulted in a form of post-traumatic stress. I
shook constantly so people were always asking if I was
cold and I was experiencing what she said were flashbacks
and these would overtake me on an almost daily basis and
made me feel violently suicidal.

There are very few places where anyone struggling with
anything like this can go for respite, if you can't afford
private care. But one day when I really feared that I was
losing my mind I had taken myself along to a place in
north London my therapist had told me about. It was
called Maytree. It said that it was a:

PADDY: Sanctuary for the suicidal where people can stay
up to four nights.

CLARE: And it was completely free. It looked just like an
ordinary house, with nice rooms for the "guests", as we
were called, and people were there to talk to you, day
and night if you needed, about how you were feeling.
There was this wonderful woman called Paddy Bazeley
who was one of the directors.

CLARE sits down by PADDY at a table, mugs in hand

PADDY: At Maytree we wanted to provide somewhere
where people can feel safe, where they can think for
a bit of time about life and death and where they can
actually talk about it. Maytree doesn't really offer
respite because it's actually hard work here. People are

encouraged to talk about what has brought them to the point of wanting to end their own lives.

CLARE: The kindness of strangers, part two.

Because I understood that my suicidal thoughts had somehow come from my childhood experiences I felt I could not share what was going on with any of my family members. After my girlfriend left me some of my friends had been as comforting and understanding as they could but when my behaviour had turned weirder, i.e. cutting myself and talking about killing myself, they had slowly but surely fallen by the wayside. As the months went by I learned the hard way that talking about feeling suicidal is clearly not an acceptable topic of conversation in our society.

(On phone to friend) Hi darling...

FRIEND: Oh dear. Are you still not feeling any better?

CLARE: I had such an awful night. At one point I went in the kitchen and got this huge knife out and I just wanted to plunge it into my heart...

FRIEND: Perhaps you should go jogging? Exercise is meant to help you when you're down.

CLARE: I'm so sorry to bother you with all this.

FRIEND: Or watch some telly. *The Commander's* on tonight, and you like Amanda Burton don't you?

CLARE: *(To audience)* But I'm sorry to say that by that point even the lovely looking Amanda Burton couldn't cheer me up. I needed to talk to my best friend but she just didn't want to listen.

PADDY: Maytree is run by a few full-time people plus something like sixty volunteers who are kind, thoughtful and interested in the guests. Very experienced in terms of being with suicidal people and who have maybe some sort of awareness of our own madness or potential for madness or depression or suicidality.

CLARE: I was at Maytree for five days. My illness eventually went on for five years so it didn't fix me as such but it did provide a little rest along the way.

PADDY: We wanted to get a balance of the place being safe in a physical sense that would reflect the safety we were offering in the psychological and emotional sense. Because suicidal people often have a fear of actually falling apart.

CLARE: Staying there gave me personal experience of what works for people like myself who feel actively suicidal on a daily basis: what can calm us down, what can lessen our fears and what can give us just a little hope to help us survive through to the next day. So why couldn't a hospital ward staffed by dozens of psychiatric nurses, presumably at a great cost to the NHS, manage to do any one of those things?

On the ward the nurses hardly spoke to us at all but, for the first time since I'd been ill, I found in some of the patients people I could really talk to about feeling suicidal. One of the closest friends I made during my time in hospital was Tony, a lovely young man from Mauritius who was twenty-seven and sweet and kind and incredibly gentle. When I first got to know him he would make comments about how:

TONY: I quite fancy Liz, you know, my named nurse? She's really fit.

CLARE: But after getting to know each other and me telling him I was gay, he eventually revealed that:

TONY: The thing is Clare, that I'm actually bisexual.

CLARE: And a little while later it came out that:

TONY: I think I'm probably completely gay but my family are strict Hindu and they don't want to accept it, so I have to pretend that I'm not.

CLARE: And after that little revelation we got on even better! There were many times when I was deeply moved and touched by his kindness.

TONY: If you get in a bad way, you must always find me. The nurses won't help you; you've got to find another patient 'cos we have to look after each other in here.

CLARE: Something that used to happen in hospital but also for a year or so afterwards was that when I was in a bad way my legs became like jelly and I would collapse on the floor...

CLARE sinks to the floor

TONY: *(Discovering her)* Oh my God, are you OK?

CLARE: Sorry, sorry.

TONY: It's all right. It's OK.

TONY helps CLARE up onto chair

CLARE: Thank you... I just couldn't get up. I can't explain it...

TONY: It's all right. You're safe now. I'll get you a cup of tea, just wait there.

ACTOR: The kindness of strangers, part three.

CLARE: Tony was a serious self-harmer. He had several long deep gashes right down both his arms. I self-harmed too, but only superficial cuts. Tony was in a league far above mine!

TONY: But you and me, we're the same, we understand each other.

CLARE: I'd only been self-harming for the last couple of years but it was such a relief to talk about it to someone else who did it too.

TONY: You know you can use your specs for cutting? Just break the glass, it's easy. Or the tops off drink cans, they're quite good as well.

CLARE: I hadn't thought of that, so they became my "cutting device of choice" while I was on the ward. You weren't officially allowed to have cans in your room for that reason, but they never checked.

TONY: And you're not allowed a plug when you have a bath in here.

CLARE: You had to stuff the plug-hole up with toilet paper.

TONY: It's so you can't drown yourself.

CLARE: Tony told me that his self-harming had started in his early teens. I asked him what had made him do it the very first time.

TONY: It was a silly thing but I just wanted to see how much I'd bleed, just a little cut. It hurt like hell, but I did it and now I live to regret it 'cos I can't stop doing it.

ACTOR: Pam Blackwood was head of operations with Samaritans between 2003 and 2009 and was also a member of the Guideline Development Group for the 2005 NICE Report on Self-Harm.

PAM: For many years I worked as a self-harm care manager in a hospital and with a lot of the people I saw, the intention was suicide, but there were people I saw whose intention was not suicide and that's the people who now we would say "self-harm".

CLARE: *(To TONY)* So were you going through a hard time when you started doing it?

TONY: When I was fifteen I told my parents I was gay and I got kicked out. They said:

PARENT: Just go. I'm not having you living under this roof.

TONY: But I didn't know where to go so I stayed on the streets. I was on drugs, heroin, cocaine, it was a nice mix! And I was raped by these men. I gave up my body to get high. But I know what those men look like, I'm pretty sure I could pick them out even though it's been so many years. I can imagine how much they've aged. I remember the scent of their aftershave, their breath, their nails, their clothes, the sound of their voices. By the time they were through with me I knew them pretty much by heart.

But later I just sank down because I had a family who refused to believe that I was gay, refused to allow me to be gay, to hear that I was sexually assaulted by men, repeatedly... They just said:

PARENT: But you're gay so why do you mind?

TONY: They don't care that it was a wrongdoing. It's like I don't have the right to say "No" because I'm gay. I'm supposed to enjoy it.

PAM: I think first of all you have to try and understand what the meaning of self-harming is for that person... So you find what is happening for that person by asking things like, "Were you trying to kill yourself?" A very common phrase with self-harm is:

ACTOR: "It's a cry for help."

PAM: But my question would be: "If you're crying out for help, what is the help you need and why do you need it?" Self-harm is a way of coping with emotional distress and emotional pain and for some people it's making the pain visible. The emotional pain is so bad that if I cut myself in some way then I've got a physical pain and that removes me from the emotional pain, and then I feel OK, until the next time. So self-harm is a survival mechanism. It's a way of staying alive in the only way that person knows at that time in their life.

TONY: I've been back at home from the age of eighteen till now, looking after my mother. She had a stroke, paralysed on the right-hand side. I've been a full-time carer and it's driven me into the ground because you have no friends, just a vicious, strict family that's never there for you.

I've got no self-respect. Just pure hatred as it's my fault I was abused. My fault for being gay. It's my fault that I took drugs. My fault that I put myself in that position. That's what I believed.

Then my mother had another stroke and I decided that
if I starved myself it would be a way of dying. So every
time I ate I vomited. And seeing my mother like that I
thought, "I haven't got the energy to look after her, I
really can't do it." My family all came to the hospital but
as soon as Mum was discharged, nobody came home to
help, and that was it. I took an overdose of paracetemol
and I slit my wrist and ended up in hospital.

Scene Four

CLARE: There was a small communal area on the ward,
near the nurses' office, where you could sit around with
other patients. Nothing much to do there but if you
got lonely in your room it was just a place to watch the
world go by. It was there I first met Debbie.

DEBBIE: Hiya.

CLARE: Is that your guitar?

DEBBIE: Yeah. Do you play?

CLARE: Yes but I'd prefer to listen to you.

Debbie sang these songs with incredible lyrics about the
dangers of established religion or how grass was better
for you than crack or about this homeless man that
she'd met once who'd died young.

DEBBIE: I started writing songs when I was a kid... when I
was lying in bed. I love the written word... the spoken
word... the sung word. And songs are the best way to get
across to people what you've got to say. I've written about
being a victim of society – and that was before I had my
bipolar – and then a lot of the songs I've written since.

CLARE: When Debbie sang and played, she would perform as if her life depended on it.

DEBBIE: *(Singing)*
Jesus was a mushroom any Christian man would eat
By taking up his body it was a psychedelic feast.
Trip on, trip on...

CLARE: To be honest, I don't think the nurses liked her music very much, but I just loved the woman's energy, her drive, her anger!

DEBBIE: On the ward sometimes you'd get a good group of patients and this particular time, we all bonded really well and we were singing and having a great time and this one night we were still at it at one o'clock. Well, the next night we thought we'd do it again but the nurses, they had it in for us, especially the staff nurse, this bloke Shamma, he weren't going to have it on his shift so we were all given pills, medicine, and we all started going down like flies. And not only did they allow it but they set that up and I thought that was wrong.

CLARE: If ever I was in distress or needed help the story was always the same...

CLARE falls down on the floor, makes a call on her mobile

Tony, it's me... I'm having a difficult time...

TONY ENTERS CLARE's room

TONY: It's all right; I'm going to get the nurse.

TONY EXITS, NURSE ENTERS

NURSE: What you doing there on the floor? Get up!

CLARE: I can't.

NURSE: *(Very firmly)* Come on, get up now!

   NURSE slowly helps CLARE up onto the bed

   There you are.

CLARE: I'm really worried that I'm going to self-harm...

NURSE: Don't be doing that now.

   NURSE EXITS room
   CLARE cuts herself and then very slowly struggles to the door
   A NURSE walks by CLARE but doesn't stop
   A MALE NURSE then comes by and notices the blood on
   CLARE's arms
   He grabs CLARE forcibly

MALE NURSE: What you done? Oh my God!

   He shoves her onto the bed roughly

   What did you use to cut? Where is it?

   He starts searching ferociously around the room
   He leaves the room and after a while comes back with a
   FEMALE NURSE

MALE NURSE: *(To FEMALE NURSE)* I see you looking at
   yourself in the mirror. Yes, you're looking good to me,
   girl!

   Both NURSES laugh and flirt together

CLARE: Can I have some Elastoplasts for the cuts?

FEMALE NURSE: No.

CLARE: What?

FEMALE NURSE: You're not having any. Here, now take one of these and go to sleep.

FEMALE NURSE gives CLARE medication

CLARE: The nurses on the ward seemed to have such a huge problem around people who self-harmed.

ACTOR: Pam Blackwood...

PAM: I think one of the difficulties is that nursing is about medicine and you might choose to specialise in psychiatry but in a way it's still about treating people with medicine and making them better and that's the reward of the job. But if there is somebody who is a revolving-door patient – and people who self-harm often are – there's a sense of impotence for some people who think, "My skills aren't helping you and therefore I feel bad."

But for others I actually think there may be something punitive and I really wouldn't want to generalise but if a nurse feels that self-harm isn't a mental illness and therefore you shouldn't be here because you're taking up a bed from somebody with schizophrenia who "I know I can do something for" then that's the thought process that actually gets them to be punitive in some way.

CLARE: On one of my ward rounds the doctor said:

DOCTOR: I hear that you've been self-harming, is that true?

CLARE: Yes, a bit.

DOCTOR: I don't want to see! Don't show me!

CLARE: And I always found that reaction a little strange. The nurses' response to my self-harming was a bit odd as well...

NURSE: What did you use to cut? Where is it? We're going to search your room.

CLARE: But for whatever reason I still needed to do it and eventually I found a way of getting them off my back.

NURSE: What have you done?

CLARE: *(To NURSE)* They're just superficial cuts and I did them yesterday.

NURSE: Oh, OK.

CLARE: Then they'd calm down and leave you alone because you had reassured them that it hadn't happened on their shift so they couldn't be held responsible.

PAM: I don't think medication will stop people self-harming. For some people maybe something that lowers that emotional temperature might be helpful but I don't think self-harm can be treated with medication.

It's about refuge. That's what people need. Self-harm is something that happens because a person is going through a number of emotions and feelings and for most people it's a way of coping with unbearable pain, which isn't a medical condition.

DEBBIE: It seems to me the nurses aren't there to care for sick people, it's almost like they're there to punish you for having a few more screws loose than them. They've got all their marbles, they've got a good job and you're in there. It becomes almost like a prison situation. There's no caring.

Scene Five

CLARE: What was so very tiring there was that in order to get the smallest of things you always had to ask a nurse first. Now to actually find a nurse was sometimes quite a feat in itself. They were usually hidden away in the office so you'd go up and down the corridor looking around till you eventually found one and then you'd get:

NURSE: Just a minute and I'll be with you.

CLARE: Which doesn't sound too rude, does it? But it was *always*:

NURSE: I said I'd be with you in a bit.

CLARE: I don't think their job descriptions actually allowed them to ever say:

NURSE: Yes of course, I'll do that for you right now.

CLARE: Or perhaps it was a power thing 'cos it would be...

NURSE: I'll do it for you later. I'm busy now.

CLARE: But my friend's come to see me. Please can you let her through the door?

NURSE: I'll go up there when I've finished what I'm doing.

CLARE: Would you lock my room while I have a bath? *(To audience)* Because there were still all these thefts going on around the ward.

ACTOR: Thieving on the ward will NOT be tolerated.

CLARE: So it said in the leaflet...

ACTOR: The Elliott Tillery Ward Leaflet!

CLARE: But the nurses did tolerate it because they took no interest if you reported that things had been stolen. If they'd even just kept half an eye out for people going into rooms where perhaps they shouldn't be, that would have helped. But you were living in constant fear of your things being nicked every time you went to the loo or to get a cup of tea. So all the time it was:

(To Nurse) Could you lock my door please?

NURSE: I will when I next go up that end.

CLARE: Excuse me, could you lock my door?

NURSE: In a minute, I'm busy just now.

CLARE: One of the best ways I found to save you running around was to just stand in the corridor outside your room hoping that a nurse might pass by at some point...

NURSE goes by

CLARE: Could you please unlock my room?

STUDENT NURSE: I'm a student nurse. I only have keys for the main doors, not for the rooms.

DOCTOR goes by

CLARE: Excuse me, could you please unlock my room?

DOCTOR: Doctors don't have keys for the rooms.

CLARE: *(To another NURSE)* Hello, could you please unlock my door? …

Nurse walks by not hearing

Excuse me?

NURSE ignores her

And then there was the business of knocking on the office door, whenever you needed something…

CLARE knocks on door. She waits and repeats and waits and repeats
Eventually a NURSE opens it:

NURSE: Yes?

CLARE: Could we have some milk please?

PATIENT: Could we have some teabags please?

PATIENT: Could I have a light please?

CLARE: Can we have some loo paper in the bathrooms please?

PATIENT: Could you get someone to unblock the toilets? There's only one loo out of four that's working.

CLARE: Hello? Could someone let me out for my leave?

NURSE: Are you sure that you've got leave?

CLARE: The consultant said I could have an hour today.

NURSE: Well, I'm going to have to check that.

CLARE waits and waits until NURSE appears again

CLARE: Excuse me, did you check my leave?

NURSE: I was busy with something else. I'll do it when I'm back in the office.

PATIENT: Do you know when my ward round is this week?

NURSE: I'll find out for you later.

PATIENT: Could you just find out what sort of time of day it might be, morning or afternoon?

NURSE: Could be anytime, you have to wait until you're called.

CLARE: Could we have some milk please?

NURSE: There'll be some coming later this morning.

CLARE: But I've got a really dry mouth from this new medication I'm on.

(Seeing some milk through the office door)

Could I use some of that milk, please?

NURSE: That's for the staff only. There's some more milk coming later for the patients.

CLARE: Can I have a teabag please?

NURSE: In a minute, I'm on the phone...

CLARE: Just one teabag please?

NURSE: *(Firmly)* You'll have to wait, we're very busy!

NURSE: She's making a call.

CLARE: *(Slightly sarcastically)* Well, do you think maybe *you* could give me a teabag then?

NURSE: If you talk to us that way you're not going to get anything!

CLARE: *(Shouting)* Do you know what? Just forget it! Just fucking forget it!

CLARE hits the door
NURSE tuts

NURSE: Shall we give you a pill to calm you down Clare? Um?

CLARE: Debbie told me that over the years she'd learnt a few things:

DEBBIE: On the wards you've got the glass door and they're on the other side of it, the nurses, the doctors, and that's where I learnt my trick which is *(Shouting)* "NURSE... NURSE!" Bang bang bang on the window.

NURSE: What is it, Deborah, what is it?

DEBBIE: That's the only way they come running out. I learnt it from this girl who used to do it just like that.

Kicking and banging and they would come running out and I thought, "I'll do that," and that's how I used to get seen. Because otherwise they'd just let you stand there politely knocking for hours and acting like you're not there.

I always used to go and check who my nurse was for that day because they're assigned to you and they've got to listen to you.

CLARE: But you could do that because you knew the system?

DEBBIE: That's from years of coming in and out.

CLARE: What was it like when you went into hospital for the first time?

DEBBIE: It was quite frightening... because it was full of nutters! It really was!

It was men and women together on the ward in those days and there were some crazy guys and girls there, so it was quite full on.

You've got your prison and then you've got your nuthouse, and there's not a lot of difference. And sometimes they put quite a lot of criminals even in the nuthouse these days because they're too mentally ill to go to prison or they've just had too much crack. Everyone's put in there. Don't matter what your mental problem is, if it's crack addicts coming down or alcoholics coming off. It's just a melting pot of people.

Scene Six

CLARE: One day this new bloke arrived on the ward...

KEVIN: Awright? How you doing?

CLARE: Yeah fine, thanks.

KEVIN: Are you a nurse?

CLARE: Yeah...

KEVIN: Oh right...

CLARE: Only joking, I'm a resident loony! *(To audience)* Most of the nurses didn't wear name badges so no-one knew who was who.

KEVIN: Oh, OK. I'm Kevin.

CLARE: Hi, I'm Clare.

KEVIN: Do you know who does drugs in here? 'Cos I can get you just about anything.

CLARE: Kevin started bringing crack cocaine and skunk on the ward every time he'd been out and, after his arrival, money started going missing.

ACTOR: Stealing will not be tolerated!

CLARE: I was getting a little worried about the whole thing because as well as the thefts and occasional violence from other patients there were now men high on crack and I started feeling really unsafe. After a lot of thought I decided to tell a senior member of the day staff about it...

NURSE: We thought that there were some drugs around and we guessed that they were coming in through him. Thank you for telling us about this. We can now search Kevin each time he comes back to the ward.

CLARE: But he had once boasted to me:

KEVIN: I don't even need to go out to get stuff. All I have to do is get my girlfriend to visit and then when she kisses me she puts it into my mouth from hers and the staff don't see nothing!

CLARE: *(To NURSE)* Please could you keep it quiet that I've talked to you about this?

I didn't really want other patients thinking I was telling the staff things because it was so often us versus them in there and we had to stick together for safety. And the other reason was that Tony had told me that Kevin was quite a well-known character on the streets of Brixton and his nickname happened to be:

KEVIN: "The Fist"

CLARE: Because of his ability to knock people unconscious from just one punch!

One night I went into Tony's room and he and this other patient were smoking crack they'd bought off Kevin and they had all this paraphernalia out to do it. Every bedroom had a glass window in the door and any nurse could have looked in and seen what they were doing. But at night-time it was quite rare for a nurse to move from their chair by the office where they'd either be reading magazines or asleep.

DEBBIE: Grass is the only drug that I take now but when I was young I was like a junkie. I had a load of acid, a lot of mushrooms, a lot of smack and a lot of speed and drinking and all that. So I'd gone from like fifteen to twenty-three as a crazy girl!

My first episode started when I had half a tab of Om, which is a type of LSD and I didn't know what was happening. It was like going completely somewhere else and I thought it was the acid that made me like that but I've spoken to a doctor since who said:

DOCTOR: No, it wouldn't have been just the acid that you took. If you've got bipolar it would have come out at some point or another.

DEBBIE: And of course it's hard on the kids. I've got five children. The oldest is twenty-two and basically they've lived with it and no-one ever explained it to them until I was put on the lithium and I had this doctor who said:

DOCTOR: Actually my brother's got bipolar...

DEBBIE: So I was like "I've got bipolar". But I wasn't getting any counselling or anything like that, even though I'd been in hospital so I didn't really know what was going on and then, once I was on the lithium, it's like because I'm taking their drug they'll bring me into their fold.

ACTOR: Dr Rufus May works as a clinical psychologist in Bradford. He was once diagnosed as a "paranoid schizophrenic" but hasn't taken any medication in twenty-one years.

DR RUFUS: I just see terms like schizophrenia or bipolar disorder as diagnoses, labels really. Whenever you put someone on a drug, all you're doing is suppressing the experience. In a holistic approach, the argument is that the illness is a release of toxins from the body, so acute illness is a way of the body attempting to release toxins. It's a way of the body trying to survive. But medical models try to battle with the illness and treat it, and if they can't treat it then they suppress the symptoms, but something else then comes along that's just as difficult to manage.

It might be apathy and hopelessness or it might be that a person puts on weight and develops diabetes and a heart condition. These are all very common effects of being on long-term psychiatric medication.

DEBBIE: Once when I was in hospital they put me on droperidol and I came out of there and got pregnant pretty quickly after being on that drug and I had a child with Down's Syndrome. And I think there's a connection but I can't prove it because it's one of those, "Hey, anyone can get it, you can't blame it on this or that."

When I went on the lithium they said it would decrease my episodes, but they didn't tell me that if I didn't take the lithium then my episodes would get worse than they ever had. Like I get seriously ill. Whereas before I might have been getting "crazy nut nut lady" now I'm getting really ill.

DR RUFUS: The problem with just giving people medication is that you teach them to be helpless, and just to rely on a pill. But if it was my son or daughter who started to hear voices or started to have manic episodes, I'd want them to kind of look at what those experiences were all about, what the meaning was. And I'd want them to be taught ways to calm down, and if medication was going to be used, I'd want it to be used very sparingly, not in a heavy-handed way. And if it didn't work, I wouldn't want the dose increased, I'd want something else tried!

DEBBIE: There was one time I went to go up to Brixton with nothing on but a sleeping bag, looked like a bloomin' caterpillar! Jumped up on a bus, dropped me sleeping bag. Then the police took me home and my boyfriend, David, who I live with, he looked after me until I got better.

DR RUFUS: If somebody were to come to me who'd been diagnosed with schizophrenia or bipolar disorder and wanted to come off medication, I would work with them carefully and sensibly at that and say, "Well, you've got to find other ways to manage your moods and I'd like you to develop those now before you come off medication, but I want you to do it gradually." I'd want them doing something like Tai Chi, yoga, something like that regularly every day. So they could create their own mental equilibrium.

DEBBIE: Before my last episode I'd just given up the lithium, 'cos I thought I was going to have a baby, and I didn't tell anyone I'd stopped taking it and then about ten days down the line I was just back into darkness.

My mental state of perception and understanding goes to other places, like when you're really enthusiastic about things as a kid. And my brain is taking me enthusiastically down a road or a path in my head but I'll just be laying there, I can't move, I'm off, I'm gone. Ga ga. Sometimes I come home and sort of shit on the floor, you know? Things that are really horrible and embarrassing for the kids. And it's twenty-four hours. You don't sleep. It's terrible 'cos you're running around, I mean, to be honest, I can't trust myself...

And that last time I rang up the police.

POLICE: Hello, you're through to the police service. Can we have your name please?

DEBBIE: Yeah, my name's Debbie, I'm on a lithium comedown, 28 Crawley Way, can you come and get me please?

POLICE: All right, stay where you are, love, we'll come and get you.

DEBBIE: Well they didn't come for ages so I put my coat on, got on the bus to go down to the hospital to check myself in and while I was doing that the police came to my house. They ripped open the back door, just ripped it open. It was locked but they broke all the locks, went upstairs, got a torch, shone it in the kids' faces.

POLICE: We're looking for Libby. Where is Libby? Are you Libby?

DEBBIE: Went in every kid's bedroom. All three of them and then David got up and had to deal with them and then finally they left, and then all the heat was off. It was like I was some IRA bomber, you know?

Scene Seven

ACTOR: On the Elliott Tillery Ward an occupational therapist runs individual and group sessions, Monday to Thursday...

CLARE: The only member of staff who spent any time with me at all was an occupational therapist called Sarah.

SARAH: *(Intensely)* Hello Clare, I'm Sarah. So Clare, at home would you say that you're able to manage your own personal hygiene?

CLARE: Yup.

SARAH: And can you cook unassisted?

CLARE: Yup.

SARAH: Can you clean your own flat?

CLARE: Yup.

SARAH: Do you have any difficulties with shopping?

CLARE: Erm... yes.

SARAH: *(Looking up and excited)* Oh really? What sort of problems exactly?

CLARE: Well there isn't a Waitrose in Tulse Hill... I mean, how's a girl supposed to manage?

I quickly discovered that the worst thing you can do to a doctor, a nurse or an OT is to suggest through a comment or even a throwaway joke that at the end of day we might all just be human beings together.

ACTOR: Dr Rufus May...

DR RUFUS: There's something about staff in institutions having to make a very clear distinction between them and the residents and there's a myth that if you actually try and communicate with people with mental health problems, you'll get it, you'll catch it! I think that in our culture we're so afraid of madness and distress because we don't ascribe any meaning to it so we're completely afraid of the unknown. So by touching someone else's, we might get in touch with our own.

CLARE: *(To DEBBIE)* The only thing I thought was good out of all the things they offered was this guy who did the fitness classes.

DEBBIE: That man was real. He got you going but it really worked.

ACTOR: Exercise classes take place on Monday morning and Friday afternoon!

CLARE, DEBBIE and EXERCISE MAN work out to music

EXERCISE MAN: That's good, that's good, ladies. I know the medication you're on will make it harder but keep going if you can... that's right, Clare... that's good, you look like you've maybe done some dance classes before?

CLARE: I had actually been in a West End musical for two years and I'd had to do a few dance routines but I thought it best not to mention...

EXERCISE MAN: That's not bad at all, Clare! Considering... that you're not even Jamaican!

CLARE: He wasn't at all patronising, like the other people running groups or the nurses. You felt with them like you had to be really stupid. It was as if they couldn't cope if you showed even the slightest sign of intelligence!

ACTOR: Dr Rufus May:

DR RUFUS: Nurses are very scared of their own distress so, by diagnosing someone, it's a defence against thinking about what it's like to be them.

In our society we have this belief that technology will sort things out and it just doesn't work with human distress.

CLARE: I can see that by pathologising mental distress, the pharmaceutical companies come off really well, but what I can't work out is why the NHS and western society in general buy into this without questioning whether there might be other ways of treating people who are mentally ill, other than by medication?

DR RUFUS: In our culture there is this thing about not wanting to look at feelings, because if somebody's feeling distressed, it must be because something unjust has happened and we don't want to look at that. We're a tough country! We went around ignoring other people's feelings by conquering and exploiting them. So our whole culture's not based on being empathetic, it's based on persuading people to give us what we want. We've got a culture that's quite macho and militaristic and it's all about repressing our emotions.

If psychiatry and the mental health services
aren't about drugging then there's no real role for
psychiatrists. If we have a holistic approach to
recovery then psychiatrists' jobs and economic power
are threatened. But the medical establishment are
in collusion with the pharmaceutical industry even
though they know in their heart of hearts that all they
are doing is suppressing people's problems.

DEBBIE: Whenever I call the Mental Health Centre, like
this morning I'd got my lithium confused and I needed
to order some more and on the phone to the staff, I go,
(Slowly) "Yeah... my lithium, I ain't got my lithium."
'cos that's how I talk to them and then they know me
then! But I'm not like that when I have a high-powered
business meeting with some music executive. I'm not
like *(Slowly)* "Hello"...

CLARE: Why is it that they have to make such a marked
line between them and us?

DEBBIE: So they can patronise you.

CLARE: But mad people aren't necessarily thick! There's
loads of famous and intelligent people who have had
some kind of mental illness...

ACTOR: Virginia Woolf, John Keats, Tchaikovsky,
Beethoven.

ACTOR: Sylvia Plath, Ernest Hemingway, Emile Zola, Balzac.

ACTOR: Mary Wollstonecraft, F. Scott Fitzgerald, Kenneth
Grahame.

ACTOR: Charles Dickens, Maxim Gorky, Winston
Churchill, Vincent Van Gogh.

CLARE: I remember when I was looking at those Van Gogh paintings in Paris thinking, "OK, so if I can see the madness in his work because I'm going a bit bonkers myself, then why is he so popular with the public in general?" Were all these other people at the museum just appreciating the colours and the form of his work or do they enjoy it because they can somehow see the madness there and is that what intrigues them and draws them in? Maybe he's just showing them something that they can all somehow recognise in themselves? But *they* weren't all mad, the general public – well some of them might have been, I suppose, just a bit, because, well they say it's one in four, don't they?

ACTOR starts counting the audience in fours, pointing to each fourth person and saying "Four" loudly

ACTOR: Shelley, Dylan Thomas, Tennyson, John Clare.

ACTOR: T.S. Eliot, Emily Dickinson, Oliver Goldsmith, Victor Hugo.

ACTOR: Henrik Ibsen, Paul Gauguin, Edvard Munch, Frideric Handel...

ACTORS EXEUNT

ACT TWO

Scene Eight

ACTOR: Gustav Holst, Mussorgsky, Rachmaninoff, Rossini, Baudelaire.

ACTOR: Robert Burns, Samuel Johnson, Michelangelo.

ACTOR: Dante Gabriel Rossetti, Hans Christian Andersen, Rupert Brooke, Graham Greene.

ACTOR: Ernest Hemingway, Joseph Conrad, Tennessee Williams.

CLARE: So we might be a bit unhinged, or distressed or even suicidal but that still doesn't make us stupid.

TONY: The nurses only thought we were stupid when it suited them. I mean they were quite happy for us to look after Claudia, weren't they?

CLARE: *(To audience)* Claudia was this patient who did act very strangely.

CLAUDIA lies on floor, hands by her side, craning her neck up. She then tries to kiss TONY on the lips and follows him around when he attempts to get away from her

For some reason I was one of the few people Claudia seemed to respond to when she got into this state.

(To CLAUDIA) Come on now, let's leave Tony alone.

TONY: Can you imagine? Patients looking after patients?

CLARE: And at night, very often Claudia would seal her mouth tight shut when the nurses approached with her medication.

CLAUDIA: Clare! Clare!

NURSE: *(To CLARE)* She's asking for you. See if you can get these pills down her. She needs to take them all.

CLARE: *(To Claudia)* Come on, come on, that's right.

Then I'd lead her to her room and put her into bed if I could and that would usually take quite a while because she was always so worked up.

TONY: And the nurses were delighted that you looked after her. Saved them the bother!

CLARE: But once it got really silly, because it was the time for nightly meds and I was trying to get Claudia to take her pills...

NURSE: *(To CLARE)* Can you get these down her?

NURSE produces another plastic cup of pills

NURSE: Here you are.

CLARE: Are these for her to take as well?

NURSE: No, those ones are *your* medication. Go on, take them.

CLARE: So I had to swallow them down and at the same time try and get Claudia to take hers! It was all very confusing and to be perfectly honest I'm not sure who ended up taking what in the end!

Scene Nine

CLARE: A few weeks into my stay a lovely Irish woman
    called Eileen joined us on the ward. She, Tony and me,
    we all got on really well. She had a brilliant sense of
    humour and was always taking the mickey out of me
    and Tony for being what she called:

EILEEN: So fucking caring all the time!

CLARE: Eileen was married to a man called Mohammed
    and they were both Muslims so she wore a hijab when
    she was in the street but not when she was at home
    or in hospital. She really wanted to be shot of both
    Mohammed and the marriage and the stress of that
    situation had often pushed her to the limit, but every
    time she tried to take her life, he was the one who
    found her and he would either call the ambulance or
    get her to hospital himself.

EILEEN: The first time I went into hospital was in 2000.
    That really would have been the start of it. They said
    that I suffer from schizoaffective disorder and severe
    depression. Took 'em about three years to work it out...
    I started taking overdoses. Didn't know why and what
    was up. My head was racing, sort of rushing, you know?

CLARE: And when you're in that state, what does it feel like?

EILEEN: Well, I chop off my hair. To look different, you
    know? Not to look the same.

CLARE: And then what's the next stage?

EILEEN: By then I would have taken an overdose. 'Cos it
    all still looks the same way. I want something to change

but it doesn't. That's what it was like the first time I took myself into hospital. It was the Sunday and I was with Mohammed and he went away for a couple of hours to buy me something and he came back and I beat him up and he said that was it, he'd had it. I was really violent. To everyone, me sister and all.

But I'm OK with the medication I'm on now and that was only luck because the ward that I was on got full one night, and they can move you around to other hospitals when that happens so I ended up at this private one and the doctor there, he checked all me medication and he changed the whole thing. But the NHS doesn't want me on it because I think it's an expensive drug, but they can all fuck off! I'm on it and I haven't been out of hospital this long in three years. But before that, every couple of weeks I'd be in hospital. Overdosing...

CLARE: And do you think it's because of how you feel about yourself and what's happened to you in your life or do you think it's a chemical imbalance in your brain, or maybe both?

EILEEN: Haven't got a clue. Couldn't answer you that!

CLARE: So you can't remember any time as a child when you felt strange in your head?

EILEEN: No, never! But I was abused for years and I didn't know that it was abuse. I didn't know. It was one of the neighbours... I thought it was just funny. He used to get on top of me, tickle me, but obviously he was getting off on it, you know? But thank God the bastard died last year! 'Cos I'll go and dance on his grave. I'll dig the bastard up. Make sure he's dead!

PAUSE

CLARE: When you came into hospital, when I met you, what had happened before then?

EILEEN: I took an overdose.

CLARE: Can you remember why you were particularly upset?

EILEEN: I forget sometimes, it just absolutely washes out of my head. I was that scared to go out, I couldn't get out of the house.

CLARE: That left you with Mohammed and no one else? So in fact to go to hospital meant that you were...

EILEEN: Around other people.

CLARE: But you wouldn't feel like going to your friends or family?

EILEEN: No, couldn't do that. I didn't want to impose myself. The only way I kind of found freedom was if I went to hospital and talked to other people, yeah.

CLARE: And when you've been in hospital what have they offered you in the way of support?

EILEEN: I went to see a psychologist once when I was in hospital. He put a timer in front of him and then he just asked stupid questions. Just a load of bullshit really, with a timer! And when the timer stopped, that was it!

CLARE: So after you took the last overdose when you ended up in Elliott Tillery, were you conscious after taking the pills?

EILEEN: I was fifty-fifty. It was a really bad overdose. This time I wanted to take my life. Just had enough. And they took me to hospital and basically hooked me to machines. I stopped breathing and they gave me brain scans and everything and my family were called.

CLARE: And after that you ended up in the ward where I was?

EILEEN: That's right.

CLARE: Had you been there before?

EILEEN: Yeah, it's a kip hole, it's shit!

CLARE: Is it worse than other places?

EILEEN: They're all as bad as each other! If you're not private, that's it! There's one hospital where they give you more pills to shut you up. You could hear people saying, "I'm going to take my own life," and they just basically said, you know, "Call us if you do."

TONY: So that's why we had to look after each other when we were in a bad way.

CLARE: Thank God we all had our mobile phones!

Reading a text message from her phone

(To TONY) Oh no, it's from Eileen...

EILEEN: Come quickly.

CLARE: *(To audience)* So we dashed over to her room and she'd cut herself really badly and there was blood absolutely everywhere, all over the bed, over the floor, everywhere.

EILEEN: Shut the door and don't let the staff see.

CLARE: We've got to stop the bleeding.

TONY: There's some loo roll here.

CLARE: *(To TONY)* You wipe it off the floor and I'll try and clean her up a bit.

EILEEN: Don't be telling anybody about this.

CLARE: But it's really bad. I think we should get some help.

EILEEN: Please don't, please. Promise me you won't?

CLARE: A few nights later, it happened again with Eileen and it was the same as before. Deep razor cuts on her arms and blood all over the place.

(To EILEEN) Listen, I'm going to get someone this time, whatever you say...

(To audience) Generally we didn't like to bother the nurses with anything but it was their job after all, not ours and sometimes the responsibility just got too much for me. The official line from them was always:

NURSE: If you feel bad you come and talk to us, OK?

CLARE: But I remember this one time when I was on the floor in my room shaking and crying...

NURSE: Are you all right?

CLARE: No.

NURSE EXITS

59

Now you might be thinking that we're not telling it as it really was. You might be thinking that there must have been some nice nurses, that perhaps I'm exaggerating a little or even misremembering it slightly. After all, I was ill at the time. But I think when you are ill you actually remember people's kindness maybe even more than at other times. And I have to tell you, since you're all here and since you're listening to my story, that during the entire length of my stay I saw no sign of any kind-hearted, sympathetic or caring member of staff on that ward, nurse or doctor. And that's for the record.

There was this other time at night that I went along to the office and found the nurse in charge.

GLADYS: Yes what is it, Clare?

CLARE: I'm really worried that I'm going to self-harm tonight. Would it be OK if you just popped along to my room every now and then and check on me please?

GLADYS: We're far too busy to do that.

TONY: Sometimes there would be no psychiatric nurses on at night, just care assistants.

CLARE: And they gave out very strong signals that they did not want to be disturbed by the patients.

TONY: Night is the most important time because that's when things go wrong with us, it's in the evening. It's when it's quiet and you start thinking and you need help and you need someone to talk to.

ACTOR: Paddy Bazeley:

PADDY: At Maytree there are always two of us here at night and we can be woken up at any time. Nights can be difficult for all of us because it's dark and you can't see and you can't do anything and there are shadows and ghosts and loneliness.

A lot of people who come here who are suicidal have had early experiences of loss, abandonment, rejection and I think that people negotiate that quite well and they get on with life and then something will happen. A relationship breaking up or whatever and they may not be conscious of it but they will suddenly become suicidal and there will be a reactivation of those feelings of isolation, worthlessness, hopelessness, lovelessness, despair, all those things. And it's despair that kills. And I suppose this is what can happen on a psychiatric ward, that you can be left on your own with it all.

CLARE: So, Eileen, that time when you were on the ward with me and you cut yourself up, did that often happen, that you felt suicidal when you were in hospital, or was that quite unusual?

EILEEN: I only did that 'cos you were all doing that! It was the fashion!

CLARE: When you first came in you said to me and Tony, and I quote: "I'd never ever do that to myself, I'm far too beautiful!"

EILEEN: Still am!

CLARE: So why did you do it?

EILEEN: Well I couldn't take an overdose, what else could I do?

61

CLARE: Ah, so it wasn't my fault!

EILEEN: And I thought, "Fuck, what am I going to do? There's too much blood!"

CLARE: And you called another patient instead of a nurse because presumably you thought we'd be nicer?

EILLEN: Yeah.

CLARE: But the second time you did it...

EILEEN: You ran for your fucking life!

CLARE: So when was the very first time you ever overdosed?

EILEEN: I was fifteen, in Ireland. I was pregnant and it was all "hush hush" and my family, they sent me to the nuns and I took an overdose there.

CLARE: Can you remember why you wanted to die?

EILEEN: To get out of the nuns. You was up at seven o'clock, saying your prayers, in bed by half past six. When I took the overdose they sent me to this hospital and they kept me there for six, seven weeks and one night I ran away. There was a group of us made a run for it and they found us and brought us back to the hospital and they gave me an injection, don't know what it was and I was pregnant and I couldn't move for about three days. We were crawling, the four of us! And they were slapping the face off me, the nurses, and in the morning it was "Get up" and I couldn't move.

So after that they sent me to a lock-up hospital and I was locked up with these really mentally

62

handicapped people and then a doctor, he called my mother and he said:

DOCTOR: Take your daughter home because there's nothing mentally wrong with her.

EILEEN: But my mother didn't want me to come home 'cos I was pregnant and my father didn't know. But in the end she said:

MOTHER: I've told your father and you can come home on the condition that you give up the baby.

EILEEN: After I had my son, they took him, the social workers and the priests and I visited him once and after that, when I was sixteen, I left for England. But then my son, he died a cot death. April 11th 1991 and I didn't find out till four months later, so they'd buried him and everything.

CLARE: After lunch one day Eileen and Tony went out together on a one-hour leave and they came back at about half past ten at night, drunk out of their skulls.

TONY AND EILEEN enter arm in arm, very drunk

EILEEN: Clare, come here, will you?

CLARE goes over to her

Tony says that you're a lesbian, is that right then?

CLARE: Erm, well yes.

EILEEN: And that you haven't got a girlfriend.

CLARE: No, no, I haven't!

EILEEN: Well give us a snog then!

CLARE: Sorry?

EILEEN: Go on, just a little kiss.

CLARE: But I thought you were married!

EILEEN: I've had affairs with women before.

CLARE: Oh really? So when was the last one?

EILEEN: When I was in hospital earlier this year, there was this woman called Lynn, we still see each other sometimes.

CLARE: Is she still in hospital?

EILEEN: No she's out now. But I'm not into her any more. It's you I want!

CLARE: So let me get this straight. You're married to Mohammed but you're really a lesbian.

EILEEN: I suppose so.

CLARE: But you only get off with women who are on psychiatric wards?

EILEEN: That's the only time I'm away from my husband! Oh go on, just one kiss, that's all I'm asking.

CLARE: Eileen, you're pissed!

EILEEN: Does that mean you'll kiss me when I sober up?

CLARE: Look, I really like you and if we were both, you

know, not mad and outside in the real world and if you weren't completely drunk and if you weren't basically straight and married to a Muslim, well then things might be different...

EILEEN: Just one little kiss and then I'll leave you alone!

CLARE: Good night Eileen! Sleep tight.

I don't know whether there was a disproportionate number of lesbians and gay men on that ward when I was in there but I must admit that it was fun to have them around, even though you could tell the staff didn't approve. Later on, a chap called Andy came onto the ward who was gay too and Tony fancied him rotten so the four of us became like a little gang and it was comforting to some extent, feeling somehow part of a group, when we'd all felt so alone for such a very long time.

EILEEN: So, if you won't snog me now will you snog me when we get out of here then?

CLARE: One night Eileen sent me a text message. I was in my bed when I got it and it went:

EILEEN: Sorry 2 say we can never B 2gether. I am crazy about U. My stomach gets all jumpy when I talk 2 U. But I luv being friends. All my friends are hard nuts and U come along being soft and great and being really funny and that makes me crazy about U. Kiss.

CLARE: And I've kept that message on my phone till this day.

Scene Ten

ACTOR: Welcome to the Elliott Tillery Ward leaflet!

Ward Round! You will be seen in the ward round once or twice a week to meet your consultant and the team.

CLARE: The ward round days were quite important, not only because of the medication prescribed each time by the consultants but also because they decreed how many hours' leave you could have. For the first week you weren't allowed outside the ward, then after that you could have one hour a day. The next step up was a four-hour leave and that was quite a big deal and you had to make a very convincing case to get one.

NURSE: Come!

CONSULTANT: Hello... Clare. And how are you?

CLARE: Yeah. OK.

CONSULTANT: *(Looking at notes)* I see that you've been making lots of friends on the ward?

CLARE: It was strange how he made that seem as if it was something bad. But I guess that patients are often so in their own worlds that having friends of any sort in that environment probably is unusual. I'd noticed that the staff seemed almost threatened if there were more than two or three of us chatting away or all going into the smokers' room at one time. But anyway, back to the job in hand.

I was wondering...

CONSULTANT: Yes.

CLARE: This Thursday evening, there's a showing of a film that I sort of made.

CONSULTANT: Oh yes?

CLARE: And I was thinking if you gave me leave then I could ask my friend to take me there and then drop me back. It's not very far away from the hospital.

CONSULTANT: We don't usually allow evening leaves.

CLARE: But it's sort of like a premiere... of the film and I've been asked to attend... because I wrote it.

CONSULTANT: I see.

CLARE: I tried to emphasise that I would return safely and swiftly after the showing but I know that they were always worried about giving longer leaves in case the patient never came back. I wasn't on a section but if you were and you didn't return when you said you would, they'd send the police out for you and patients would sometimes appear back on the ward escorted by coppers. But I think what persuaded them was when they asked:

CONSULTANT: So where exactly is this film being shown?

CLARE: Er... Scotland Yard.

CONSULTANT: What?

CLARE: It was made for Age Concern but it's also being sponsored by the Metropolitan Police.

CONSULTANT: Erm, well yes, in that case, yes, all right you can go.

CLARE: Now I may be wrong but I don't think they had had too many requests before of that nature.

And when the evening came I got all dressed up in a suit that a friend had brought me from my flat. And we both went to the film showing and for nearly three hours I tried to come across to everyone there as relatively normal. I found it all very tiring and when my mate dropped me back on the ward...

CLARE's friend hugs her goodbye and EXITS as NURSE locks the doors. CLARE then goes to sit on her bed

PATIENT: *(Shouting)* Nurse? Nurse?

PATIENT: Shut up, I'm trying to sleep!

CLARE: Now I don't believe in fairytales but at that moment, sitting on my bed I felt just like Cinderella at midnight...

I got on with most of the patients there but there was one woman I had a huge problem with. Her name was Susan and I clearly recall the night they brought her up to the ward...

SUSAN is in handcuffs and she is shouting and kicking and spitting at a policeman

I remember thinking in a rather detached – as if I was watching some reality TV – sort of a way: "Well, this one should liven things up around here!" because she was, shall we just say, quite a colourful character!

It soon became very clear that Susan fancied Tony...

TONY: Nah, she doesn't fancy me!

CLARE: Tony, she fancies you!

TONY: She just comes in my room sometimes for a chat.

CLARE: Yeah, 'cos she fancies you!

TONY: She's OK really. Come and talk to her and you'll see.

CLARE: So I did. I tried to be friendly with her but she didn't like it that I was so close to Tony. Her exact words as I recall being:

SUSAN: Tony doesn't want to fuck you 'cos you've got a dirty pussy.

CLARE: I restrained myself from mentioning that the main reason why Tony didn't want to fuck me was because he was a poof and I was a dyke.

(To TONY) She just hates it that we're always together and cuddling each other.

TONY: There's no way I'd be as physical with a straight woman as I can be with you.

CLARE: And it was so important to me, that closeness that I had with Tony.

TONY: Susan will be cool about it soon, you'll see.

SUSAN: *(To CLARE)* I hope that God gives you more scars and cuts on your arms.

CLARE: One day she came up behind me with a glass of near boiling water and was just about to throw it over me when...

TONY: Clare, watch out!

TONY knocks the glass out of SUSAN's hand

CLARE: Oh my God, I didn't even see her there.

TONY: Wow, that was a close thing!

CLARE: And there was a member of staff who saw the whole incident... and said nothing.

Mary, however, was a patient that I got on with very well. She was an older woman with long grey hair and I knew she listened to Radio Three because her room was opposite from mine. I remember the first time we met had been a little on the surreal side.

MARY: You look just like that lady off the telly, who does radio work, you know?

PAUSE

She's famous. You know? erm, Sandi something?

CLARE: Sandi Toksvig?

MARY: Yes, that's her! Well she's not really famous. Is that you?

CLARE: No, my name's Clare, but I do actually know Sandi.

MARY: Yes. I know Tom Cruise. In fact he used to be a lover of mine and now he owes me money. And I was a personal friend of Henry the Eighth.

CLARE: *(To audience)* One very important lesson to learn on a psychiatric ward is not to name drop. You will never be believed.

After we both left hospital we stayed in touch and one thing we agreed on was how stupid the questions were that they asked us in the ward rounds!

MARY: To ask a person what your "mood" is is crazy! I've been diagnosed as schizophrenic and manic depressive but I'm a pianist too, and with music it varies all the time, doesn't it? From a great crashing fortissimo on the piano to a pianissimo passage.

CLARE: Had you been into hospital before?

MARY: Many times.

CLARE: How many?

MARY: About twenty at least because I know about the realm around us that the angels inhabit and other beings, and I relate to that world and it has got me into trouble with people who don't believe it exists. They call it "hearing voices" and they call it "mental illness"...

CLARE: And you call it?

MARY: Well, communing with angels really. I suppose I have got an illness but I do relate to the other side, the world around us that people can't see and hear, and they call that "nuts".

When I was little I saw an angel but there are a lot of psychics like me that have this problem with the mental health system, we don't fit in.

Because, "I heard this voice say to me"... well that's like a red rag to a bull for a psychiatrist and they'll say:

CONSULTANT: Right, you're hearing voices, double the medicine!

MARY: But I don't think that I'm ill. I think the spirits are all around people and I can see them and hear them sometimes. But I've learnt not to tell psychiatrists much about what I'm thinking or hearing. Don't trust them. And when I was in hospital they closed the world of angels, closed it all up with the drugs.

And the medication stops me having visions and feeling high. I think hearing voices is spiritual awareness and their bloody medicine makes you subnormal. If you can see an angel, it makes you really happy! My son thinks I'm really well when I'm zapping along interacting with him. When I take the drugs I'm a zombie and I can't reply properly. My kidneys are in a terrible state because of the sodium in the drugs but they dish them out like sweets! But you're not told about the side effects. But it's all pill pill pill pill and the pills can be dangerous for you and people die much earlier on these pills: that's what's been found. But a lot of the drugs are British so the British medicine system is like a huge dinosaur feeding on us.

CLARE: Do you ever feel better in hospital than you do at home?

MARY: I hate being in there but sometimes it feels better because sometimes at home is dreadful.

CLARE: So it's the lesser of two evils?

MARY: Yeah. Hearing things on that level that can be so very harmful.

CLARE: But initially you had a good experience in that world?

MARY: I didn't relate to it too much because I was bringing up a child and I had a job. I was a secretary in the civil service. I was a teacher before that and an arts administrator before that. But because I was hearing and seeing things I was so frightened that my husband was going to steal my son away from me if I didn't get on with him.

CLARE: Did you love your husband at all?

MARY: A bit, yeah. So I went on living with him until he divorced me and then he up and left and it's very hard on his son because he doesn't even know where his dad is.

CLARE: Do you think that talking to someone in hospital about your personal experiences would ever help?

MARY: Definitely. Definitely it would help.

CLARE: So if you were in charge of a ward, what three main things would you like to see changed there?

MARY: I think I'd move the violent patients to another ward and employ more caring nurses and I'd try more verbal therapy.

Scene Eleven

CLARE: Hospital is no place for an ill person.

As the weeks went by I realised that however much I
hated that place, I was scared of leaving it too. I now
knew that whatever I was going through was not just
a depression thing. It felt as if the wheels had well
and truly fallen off. In the two months that I spent on
that ward, no member of staff ever asked me why I felt
suicidal or why I had taken an overdose or why my
legs seemed to give way when I was distressed. They
never asked me where my terrifying flashbacks might
be coming from or why I felt the need to self-harm so
often. Patients were confined and medicated and that
was all.

ACTOR: Dr Rachel Perkins:

DR RACHEL: I do think that some people want talking
therapy and that should be available. Clearly it's one
of the things that we should be offering as a health
service, but I think we have to start from the principle
of humanity and actually take an interest in people's
lives. And I don't really call that therapy, I call that
being human. When you go into hospital, someone to
actually sit down with you, have a cup of tea and say:

NURSE: How did you get here? I expect it must have been
horrible for you recently. So, you've been brought here
by the police and that must have been shitty...

CLARE: What do you think it is about the staff that makes
them not be able to ask in, as you say, this very human
way, ask people about themselves?

DR RACHEL: I think it's two things. One, that they can't regard patients as people and the other thing is that when you train someone as a mental health professional you stop them being a person. I was a clinical psychologist before I developed mental health problems and with psychologists and therapists, we develop models for understanding why people think and feel the way they do but they're not models by people who have had those experiences.

CLARE: To be honest, I found the standard of care that the patients were given by the nurses to be absolutely shocking.

DR RACHEL: The staff will regard someone who's got mental health problems as being other and different and it's very easy for staff in hospitals, particularly on acute wards, to preserve their own status by believing that there's all this riff-raff that's completely "other". And I think that's really manifested when you've got separate staff and patient toilets.

Well, if the toilets, or indeed the crockery and cutlery, are not fit for staff to use, what right have you got to expect anyone else to use them – unless of course you see me as a lesser being who requires lower standards?

CLARE: It always confused me when Alison would say:

ALISON: I just feel better in hospital than I do at home.

CLARE: Do the nurses or doctors ever talk to you when you're on the ward?

ALISON: Angela arranged a meeting once and called me into this room for a chat with her 'cos she was my named nurse and she started asking me:

ANGELA: Have you cleaned your teeth today?

ANGELA closes her eyes

ALISON: I can see it's obviously past your bedtime.

ANGELA: I always fall asleep about this time in the afternoon.

CLARE: *(To ALISON)* So do you think that if you leave hospital for good you might feel suicidal again?

ALISON: Yes.

CLARE: And on your first admission, did you feel suicidal then?

ALISON: No, just depressed. I wanted someone to look after me.

CLARE: But that's when you jumped in the river?

ALISON: Yes.

CLARE: Can you remember the very first time you heard voices of any kind?

ALISON: I was staying with a friend of mine down in Dorking and I heard voices then.

CLARE: What did they say?

VOICE: Talk dirty to me.

ALISON: That was the first thing they said.

CLARE: And do you answer them?

ALISON: No, I was disgusted by them. I do answer them, him, now. He says it's just one man. It's always a "He", never a woman. But at one time there were two hundred men. But the voice I've got at the moment, he's not too bad. He just gives me orders.

CLARE: Like?

ALISON: Well, he can read my mind so he knows what I'm going to do. So if I'm going to open a newspaper he says:

VOICE: Go and read a newspaper.

ALISON: And if I'm going to the loo he'll say:

VOICE: Use the toilet by the dining room.

ALISON: Just directions like that.

CLARE: And now you're used to the voices do they not shock or surprise you any more?

ALISON: Not really, 'cos I've been with them for so long.

CLARE: So when there's more than one voice, are they in different tones?

ALISON: No, they're the same tone. When I'm very depressed they're difficult to counteract. Like I would be out shopping and the voices said there were twenty thousand tarantulas in my flat. I was scared. I don't like spiders anyway and the thought of any tarantula, let alone twenty thousand, was enough to keep me out and I'd stay out until someone would reassure me that it was all right to go back home.

CLARE: When you're feeling a little better do you hear the voices less?

ALISON: No, they're still around. Well, he says:

VOICE: I'm around all the time but I don't speak to you all the time.

CLARE: One evening in her room I had a conversation with Alison just after I was given my discharge date.

(To ALISON) So have you sorted out anything yet with the doctors about how long you'll be here?

ALISON: I don't really want to go back to my flat yet.

CLARE: I'm sorry but I know I won't be able to come back here again even to visit, but I could pop round and see you at your place.

ALISON: Yeah, it'd be nice to meet up.

CLARE: If we're both still alive that is!

ALISON: Well, I won't try and kill myself again if you won't.

CLARE: I can't be making promises I might not keep!

ALISON: No I mean it. If you don't try to kill yourself then I promise I won't.

PAUSE

So is it a deal?

CLARE: *(To audience)* And do you know what? I just couldn't make that promise. I wanted her to keep her

78

side of it so badly, but I just couldn't promise not to kill myself even though it would mean that someone else wouldn't die.

Scene Twelve

ACTORS sing an extract from IN THE BLEAK MIDWINTER

CLARE: It was coming up to Christmas, never the best time of year for the lonely, mad or suicidal, but suddenly the doctors started declaring that almost everyone on our ward was well enough to leave. I thought it slightly odd that several patients that I knew had been trying to get out for weeks were now all being given a completely clean bill of health. Coincidentally, I'm sure, that very week I was told by one of the nurses that there was going to be a serious staff shortage over the Christmas and New Year period and that agency staff would have to be employed by the NHS at extortionate rates.

ACTOR: The Elliott Tillery Ward offers "MOVING ON" group sessions with the occupational therapist.

CLARE: So I went along to one. Tony was there but having a bad day and refusing to join in. Susan sat down for a while and then spent the rest of the session getting up, going out and then coming back in again. There was a woman called Yvonne who used to be a patient on the ward but had now "moved on", which actually meant that she was living in a B&B, but she was so lonely there that she'd come along to the hospital each day where she was allowed to have some lunch and then she'd sit without speaking in the communal area or join in a group if she could. Sarah, the OT, had brought a flip board along with her! She'd made a chart entitled:

SARAH: "Coping with decision making." Now, does anyone have any difficult decisions that they're struggling with at the moment about their home life perhaps... that they would like to discuss? Maybe about something that needs to be done on their flat or... well anything at all like that?

Tony? ... No? Yvonne?

YVONNE: I hate where I'm living.

SARAH: Oh dear...

YVONNE: They throw you out after breakfast and you can't go back till the evening, then I just watch TV and go to sleep. Nobody talks to you.

SARAH: Right.

YVONNE: I want to come back here.

SARAH: But you can't Yvonne! You've got your own place now.

YVONNE: Um...

SARAH: So... Tony?

TONY: What?

SARAH: What have you got planned for when you leave?

TONY: I haven't got anywhere to live except with my mother where I have to be her full-time carer.

SARAH: I see... um... What it says here is "Coping with decision making". Let's have a think about, say, what you would do if you went to your fridge and it was empty?

CLARE: *(To audience)* So I was thinking, is this a trick question? 'Cos it can't be as simple as it sounds.

PAUSE as SARAH waits for replies.

SARAH: Clare? What would you do?

CLARE: Erm... Go to the shop and buy something... if I had some money?

SARAH: Good! Thank you. Now that's an example of a problem that can be solved immediately! Let's write that down... "Go to the shop and buy something."

CLARE: *(To audience)* Phew! This was going to be easier than I thought!

SARAH: So now... let's think of an example of a problem that might be solved at a later date... Tony? ... Yvonne? ... Can you think of an example?

CLARE: *(To audience)* She wasn't going to ask me this time, I could just tell!

SARAH: Well, an example of something that might be solved at a later date could be, say, if something in your home was broken and you had to arrange to fix it. Like if the heating didn't work, you'd have to call up the landlord and tell them to send someone round to mend it. *(Writing)* Heating to be fixed. Good. Excellent! Right, now, the third category of problem...

CLARE: I was getting quite excited now. She'd missed me out once; surely she'd ask me again this time?

SARAH: Can anyone think of an example of a problem that can *never* be solved? Yvonne? Tony? No? ... Clare?

CLARE: Afghanistan?

I was quite disappointed that she didn't write that one up on the board but I had gained a lot from the session. I now knew for sure that it was time for me to get the hell out of this awful place before I really did lose what was left of my mind. I had to face whatever had taken me to this point and either somehow conquer the madness or try to take my life again – but this time do it properly and not make any stupid last-minute calls that meant that I could ever end up in a place like this again.

Scene Thirteen

CLARE: Over the weeks the situation between myself and Susan had progressively worsened. Her bullying was relentless. She would pinch my arm really hard any time she went by me, pull my hair, turn the telly off if I was watching it. Switch the lights off as she went out of a room and leave me in the dark. Really little things, but enough to make me highly stressed.

ACTOR: Aggressive behaviour towards others will NOT be tolerated.

NURSE: *(Very meekly)* Don't you be doing that now, Susan.

CLARE: The day before I was due to leave she was pushing her way forward in the queue for dinner and in doing so actually knocked Alison right over onto the floor.

(To SUSAN) What the hell do you think you're doing?

Before I tell you what happened next, can I just explain that I am a pacifist. I have been all my life. I have never used violence and I believed that it was not in me to ever do so. But seeing my friend being pushed over by that bully who just laughed at me when I challenged her, well I don't know what it was but I just saw red and the next thing I knew I went up to Susan and...

CLARE slaps SUSAN

I'm not proud of what I did. I feel ashamed even telling you this part of the story. I still don't know why I resorted to physical violence. It might have been to do with the fact that I had been bullied abusively in my childhood and I was now trying to fight back, or at least defend my friend. It might have simply been a reaction to all those weeks of watching Susan getting away with terrorising myself and other patients. But whatever the reason, I did something that I'm sure I would never have done in any other place or time of my life.

And I know that I shouldn't say this, being a pacifist and everything... so don't tell anyone will you? But do you know what? When I actually slapped her, it felt... bloody brilliant!

But then, of course, came the retaliation...

SUSAN punches CLARE in the face
CLARE is sent hurtling to the floor
NURSE rushes over to both of them

NURSE: Susan, what on earth do you think you're doing?

CLARE: I quickly realised that no-one had actually seen me strike the first blow, not even Alison.

NURSE: *(To CLARE)* Go into the office and call the police. You should report this as an assault.

CLARE: Seriously?

NURSE: Because it was so violent and we don't know what to do with her any more so we think you should tell the police.

CLARE: The idea appealed to me greatly. Maybe at last Susan would get her come-uppance. But I still wasn't sure so I went to my room and called up a magistrate friend of mine who said:

FRIEND: I don't think you'd be wise to take this any further, just get out of there tomorrow and forget about the whole thing, honestly.

CLARE: I could tell that my friend thought that I was thinking irrationally but she was on the outside. I was inside a locked ward and this was the world I now knew. I had been confined with this horrible woman for many weeks and I had found no way to either ignore her cruel behaviour or to stop it. The nurses had tolerated and allowed it and never once intervened. My face was still smarting from Susan's punch so I went into the office, called the police, as I had been told to, and reported the incident.

That night when I went to bed I found that my mattress and bedclothes were completely soaked through. Susan had obviously poured water on them. There were no spare beds or mattresses and rather than sleep on the concrete floor I decided to cover the top of the bed with as many towels as I could find. It was not the best night's sleep I'd ever had.

The next day was the day I was to be discharged. But early in the morning before I was even up, the police knocked on the door of my room.

POLICE: We need to talk to you, Miss Summerskill.

CLARE: I quickly got dressed and then told them what had happened with Susan (excluding the bit about my slap of course) and how the staff had told me to report it to them.

POLICE: Yes, but you have no obvious injuries, do you?

CLARE: Not really, but it was a pretty hefty blow.

POLICE: If it had been a stab wound for example...

CLARE: I only called you up because the staff told me to.

POLICE: If such an assault had happened outside the building on the street, well then yes, you could prosecute the person in question.

CLARE: Oh, so I lose my basic civil rights now, do I, because I'm a psychiatric patient, is that correct?

POLICE: And the girl is actually on a section, so she can't be prosecuted anyway.

CLARE: How come the staff hadn't known that or explained that to me?

POLICE: So we can't proceed with this complaint.

CLARE: I'm sorry if I've wasted your time but would you please explain to the staff everything you've told me.

Well, they didn't. They just left. But I was so wound up by then. Still reeling from the events of the night before, terrified of going back to my flat and living there alone, worried about facing Christmas in this frame of mind and just generally in an incredibly anxious state. Sarah popped her head round my bedroom door to tell me that she was doing a relaxation class down the corridor and did I want to join in?

Well, do you know what? I felt that I *did* need a little relaxation so I went along there and really tried to unwind a bit, but as soon as I left the session...

SUSAN: I think you might find a few things missing from your room.

CLARE: So I dashed down there, cursing myself for having forgotten to ask a nurse to lock my flipping door, only to discover that my shoes had disappeared, along with my radio, my glasses, my clock and a few other things. I looked out of the window and saw them all broken and getting wet on the roof of another building below.

ACTOR: Thieving will NOT be tolerated!

CLARE: From that moment until I left the ward I just sobbed and sobbed and sobbed. I was still like that when I was taken into my final ward round and the consultant asked me:

CONSULTANT: We're a little concerned about letting you go home like this? You seem a bit upset.

CLARE: Of course I'm upset! If I was just a normal citizen and I'd been assaulted and robbed you'd be offering me victim support!

CONSULTANT: Perhaps you might like to stay here one more night?

CLARE: *(Very slowly)* Not if my life depended on it.

ACTOR: Finally we hope your stay will be as smooth and comfortable as possible. Above all we need to have respect for others on the ward, patients and staff. Bear in mind that you will be sharing an enclosed space with a diverse group of people. At times we all need our own space to breathe and think...

CLARE tears the leaflet up

CLARE: So that was it, time to go. Goodbye Elliott Tillery, goodbye hospital. My stay on that ward had been terrifying in so many ways but it was never the behaviour of the so-called mad people that really shocked me, because I knew that they were ill and disturbed and distressed, it was the treatment I received at the hands of the so-called carers that I'm still trying to make some sense of.

ACTOR: Dr Rufus May:

DR RUFUS: Helping somebody who's in a lot of distress is hard work, so you need very special skills to just sit there with someone's pain and still remain optimistic and compassionate – and that's just not in nurses' training.

ACTOR: Paddy Bazeley:

PADDY: Suicidal people tend to feel hopeless so it's all about the transfusion of hope. You don't have to cheer people up and you don't want to give them false hope. It's got to be genuine but I think it's something you have inside you that you can give to someone else.

CLARE: I shall remember how, in order to do their jobs each day, the nurses seemed to have to make us, the patients, far "madder" than we were, or more to the point far madder than *they* were.

DR RUFUS: Madness is a creative way of dealing with pain. Brutalising someone does not help them. We need to listen deeply to people in crisis and we need to question the idea that chemical changes are the main cause of emotional changes. If Arsenal lose to Tottenham I will experience a deep sinking feeling. This will probably be reflected by chemical changes in my brain but they did not cause this. Football players did, combined with my attachment to Arsenal!

I would argue that medicalising and numbing our pain does not help. It mystifies its meaning in our lives and ignores the social and psychological avenues to making our lives more fulfilling.

ACTOR: Dr Rachel Perkins:

DR RACHEL: The views about mental health problems that exist in psychiatric services are exactly the same as those that exist outside. If our culture believes that people with mental health problems aren't fit to do certain things then you've got people going into those services who have those views and if people with mental health problems are devalued then so are the people who work with them.

CLARE: So, according to my medical records I am now officially someone who has had:

VOICE: "Mental health problems."

CLARE: Actually, I wouldn't mind just saying that I was "ill". Isn't being ill the same thing as having a "health problem"? And when I finally left...

ACTOR: The Elliott Tillery Ward...

CLARE: I certainly wasn't ready to live on my own again but on that day I was just so delighted to finally escape from that ward because, especially near the end of my stay, my time there had felt like a prison sentence.

For several months afterwards I had nightmares about things that had happened in there, but eventually I recovered, firstly from my time in hospital and then later from my breakdown. And now, well it's all just become a story that I'm telling about something that occurred three years ago now, about a time when I sort of lost the plot. A period of my life when I went a little bonkers, a touch doolally, I was a bit out to lunch, away with the fairies.

But I'm OK now! I'm almost completely mended. Nearly back to normal. I'm one of you again, one of us, not one of them. But let me just say that in my experience, there's a very, very thin divide.

My friend came by that day to drive me home but just as I was going, a nurse who I had never seen before came up to me with a pen and notebook in hand and said:

NURSE: What do you want me to write?

CLARE: Sorry?

NURSE: What do you want me to write down here?

CLARE: Write down where?

NURSE: You are leaving, yes?

CLARE: Yes... so?

NURSE: *(Almost shouting)* So what... do... you... want... me... to... put?

CLARE: I really don't know what you're talking about.

NURSE: *(To CLARE's FRIEND)* What does she want me to write?

FRIEND: I'm so sorry but we haven't the foggiest idea what you're on about.

CLARE: It turned out that she was meant to be writing up some sort of notes about how I'd been during that shift. But I'll always remember the way she looked at me and talked to me as if I was an imbecile and how she then turned to someone who she thought wasn't mad for a sensible reply.

NURSE: Now remember that the home treatment team are going to come and visit you tomorrow morning. This is your medication, let's just check *(looking at pill packages)* yes... "Clare Summerskill".

CLARE packs up a small bag of her belongings
The other ACTORS recite the following names looking at other pill packages with names on

ACTOR: Claude Monet, Toulouse-Lautrec, Sylvia Plath, Franz Kafka.

ACTOR: Winston Churchill, Judy Garland, Cole Porter, Marilyn Monroe.

ACTOR: Audrey Hepburn, Paul Simon, Kate Millett, Laurence Olivier.

ACTOR: Joan Rivers, Stephen Fry, Roseanne Barr, Jackson Pollock.

ACTOR: Tammy Wynette, Kurt Cobain, Ellen DeGeneres, Alastair Campbell.

ACTOR: Elton John, Lou Reed, Anthony Hopkins, James Taylor.

ACTORS EXEUNT